The Soaring Single

Living as an Intentional, Purposeful Christian Single

by
Sarah C Aderibigbe

Kingdom
Publishers

The Soaring Single

Copyright© Sarah Aderibigbe

All rights reserved. No part of this book may be reproduced in any form by photocopying or any electronic or mechanical means, including information storage or retrieval systems, without permission in writing from both the copyright owner and the publisher of the book. The right of Sarah Aderibigbe to be identified as the author of this work has been asserted by her in accordance with the Copyright, Designs and Patents Act 1988 and any subsequent amendments thereto. A catalogue record for this book is available from the British Library.

All Scripture Quotations have been taken from the King James Version of the Bible

ISBN: 978-1-911697-74-9

1st Edition by Kingdom Publishers, London, UK.

You can purchase copies of this book from any leading bookstore or email contact@kingdompublishers.co.uk

Contents

SECTION 1 – DISCOVERING PURPOSE 7

1. In the Beginning 8
2. The Imprint of Destiny 17
3. The Treasure of Discovery 27

SECTION 2 – UNDERSTANDING SINGLEHOOD 37

4. The Glory of the Young 38
5. The Necessity of Interim Singlehood 47

SECTION 3 – MAXIMIZING SINGLEHOOD 57

6. Write the Vision: Read & Run 58
7. The Unseen Seed, the Seen Fruit 66
8. Single and Saturated with God 74
9. The Armoury of Planning 80
10. Singles of Substance 88
11. In Quietness and Confidence 97

SECTION 4 – THE NEXT PHASE TO CONSIDER 105

12. From Single to Spouse 106

SECTION 5 – THE SOARING SINGLE – CONCLUSION 117

13. Summary Remarks 118

To Jesus Christ, the Owner of my existence.

To my Husband, Pastor Engr. Ade Aderibigbe. May Heaven reward your tireless love, leadership and commitment to purpose.

For our beloved Children. May your generation witness the brightness of your rising. Shine strong, bright and true for Jesus Christ.

SECTION 1

DISCOVERING PURPOSE

1

IN THE BEGINNING

There was a beginning before your beginning. In that beginning which precedes your own, at some indiscernible point in eternity, you were discussed. You were discussed by the Being that created the Universe, the God of Heaven. The curious mystery here is that whether your parents planned or prayed for you, or not, God ordained your existence.

Your parent may have not even been a Bible-believing Christian nor may they have acknowledged the existence of God. You may have been found by the wayside as a baby, seemingly abandoned. You may have had a tumultuous upbringing. You may also have not. The circumstances of each individual's arrival on earth cannot be summarily exhausted in these few lines. But what can be summarily stated is that whoever you are, reading this, God intended for you to be here. But what does this actually mean?

The God of the Universe is an intentional God. He has an intention for allowing any and every given event under the sun and has an intention behind disallowing a given event. Sometimes God may reveal to us His intention for a particular occurrence, other times He may not. Being an intentional God means that nothing occurs by coincidence. He calculates, He considers, He plans, He orchestrates, He executes. God's calculations and ultimate executions correspond, not to our own elected route, but to His supreme counsel.

His counsel has factored into it all possible circumstances you have encountered and will encounter in the journey of life. This is so because of God's attribute of omniscience. The Almighty God has all knowledge which means that nothing is beyond His awareness or counsel. As natural human beings we do not have this nature of knowing all things which means we tend to attribute what we cannot explain to coincidence, luck or chance.

Occurrences can take one unawares because our foreknowledge as humans is limited: we know and see in part. However, when we begin to walk with, and begin to know, the intentional God one begins to change perspective. When we begin to attune our lives and existence to Him, a paradigm shift occurs, and we arrive at the understanding that nothing 'just happens'. The sun did not just happen. The earth did not just happen. And neither did you.

The aforementioned discussion between the three personalities of God resulted in an agreement that a being would be fashioned, with specific tendencies, peculiarities and distinctive features that would make that being like no other creature on earth. That being, of course, is you. These distinctive features include physical features, personality features, genetic features amongst others. It is a curious wonder that you are your own original custom-built creation, and no one was crafted to be completely identical to you. With all the billions of souls that inhabit the nations of the earth, no two are entirely the same. Such is a remarkable testament to the infinite craftsmanship and artistry of God.

This means each soul is a product of God's divine and glorious template fashioned with God's distinct blueprint. Allowing the awareness of this truth to sink deep into our consciousness will point us to another truth, which is that it is ultimately only in God, man's Source that we attain the true depth of all that God's heavenly blueprint encompasses.

In addition to God's original intention to create you, there are also additional dimensions that were at play. It could be that God's eyes ran to and fro' your family and a unique need was identified. In other words, your coming forth may have been Heaven's response to a need of some kind that required a resolution. In the Bible, the burdened and sorrow-laden sighing of an oppressed nation precipitated the coming forth of a deliverer in the form of the man of God named Moses. God may have orchestrated your arrival as a means of hearkening unto the sighing of a soul or a nation of souls around you whom He has identified. Perhaps someone's yearnings have come up to form a memorial before God and this translated to your birth.

We oftentimes see life and lifetimes in intervals of days, weeks, months and years, but God sees beyond that. God also sees in greater intervals of generations, lineages, centuries and eras. He can zoom out, as it were, and see the full picture of the map. He can also zoom in and see a specific region. As He does this, He has the power to design and re-design, order and re-order, shape and re-shape events all at the same time. He can change the trajectory of a generation and change the course of a nation at the stroke of His finger. When we consider this more deeply, we discover that we cannot fully and sufficiently fathom the complexity and mastery of God's workings. To attempt to unravel such workings becomes an inherently futile exercise.

There are billions and billions of human souls all over the world. God is working on each of our stories from inception and He is not constrained by resources. At any one point in time and eternity, He can be fashioning in the north, crafting in the east, ordaining in the west and bringing to birth in the south, all at the same time. This simultaneous synergy of God is another fundamental testament to the fact that our existence starts and finds its essence in the Author of our existence.

When we understand these aforementioned attributes of God, particularly His intentionality, it leads us to immediately discard the false notion that one is a mistake of some kind or a blip in creation. Arming oneself with key realities about who we are, our origin and the investment poured into us by God is crucial to opening up one's mind to the concept of divine purpose.

After the question of your existence and the schematics of your being were discussed, the topic of purpose was then also delved into, which will be treated in the next chapter. The discussion could have taken an hour, a day, a week, a year. God's language of time is not in human terms. The Bible records that a thousand years are like a second in the sight of God.

However long the project of your existence was discussed, the timing component of your arrival was finalised and sealed by God. The precise moment when the modalities of conception took place was not a coincidence, by chance or a biological accident, it was a timed and pre- ordained event. The timing element of when you would be conceived was not an exercise in arbitrariness by God, but it was an exercise in perfection.

We live life in a forward motion but oftentimes we find its beauty in hindsight which is itself backward-facing. Many-a-time we discover the subtle beauties in the timing of specific happenings much later when we look back from the vantage point of our present. We discover the ingenuity of God when we see how events in our lives eventually unfolded in a manner coordinated expertly by God. In looking back from the vantage of the present, we see the tests that came before the triumphs, the weeping that came before the winning and all manner of circumstances that morphed us into a better version of ourselves. Whilst life makes better sense looking backwards for man, for God He can reach right into any second in the continuum that is time and install an event, a change, a life. In this wise, you are no exception. The all-knowing God looked into the ages, centuries, decades, years, months, weeks and pinpointed a singular day of a specific week, month and year in the which you would be formed and eventually born.

We oftentimes celebrate the day of our birth and refer to it as our birthday. We may attribute to that day a significance, a meaning, a special status and we go to, at times, extraordinary lengths to mark and celebrate it. But we were birthed in God's heart long before that day of birth on earth. We were always in God. Somewhere in the awesomeness of His Being was some virtue in Him that would be translated into a glorious soul. Having examined the impossibility of you being an afterthought, coincidence or mistake, the notion that you matter to God should at this point now be seen to be an understatement. The understanding that you were a premeditated project that was planned, purposed and packaged by God, at this point should be real and alive in you.

Mankind happens to be the only creature that has a soul, created in God's very own tripartite image with supremely intelligible faculties. It is man that God chooses to have a relationship with, to fellowship with Him and give His spirit unto. But this relationship is not a sweeping generalised relationship with humanity, as a whole. There is also a unique, distinct relationship that He has with each and every one of His children, on such a level that God can make you feel that all His attention is on you and you alone. Your story even before it began, was special in the sight of God and therefore, it was deemed necessary by the Heavens that your story be told and played out. Understand this, engage with it and run with it.

A basic awareness of God will recognise that God's attributes are multi- faceted and perfect. All around us we see the handiwork of a supreme and perfect God. If He is intentional about the existence of the birds of the air, the flowers of the field and ensures that natural processes are set in motion to ensure their existence is secured and preserved, much more is it so for man. God does not suddenly become non-intentional when it comes to creating man.

* * *

Questions to Ponder

1. Do I recognise that I am an Intentional work of creation by an Intentional God?

2. Have I ever felt that my life and existence was a mistake? If I did feel this, why and when did this feeling arise?

3. What yardsticks have I used to define my worth?

Scripture Corner

"Before I formed you in the womb, I knew you..." - Jeremiah 1:5 (KJV)

Declaration: I acknowledge that my existence was intentionally designed by God. Despite the circumstances of my birth and my battles with self- worth and self-esteem, I make a choice to believe. I choose to believe that my existence was Heaven's discussion agenda in some point in eternity. I believe that I matter to God, and I am not present on earth by chance or accident but as a premeditated divine project of God.

-: CHAPTER 1 HIGHLIGHT: -

"When we begin to attune our lives and existence to God, a paradigm shift occurs, and we arrive at the understanding that nothing 'just happens'."

NOTES

2

THE IMPRINT OF DESTINY

Destiny, purpose, calling. These are words oftentimes thrown around. They are words uttered much more often than they are pondered upon. Perhaps by virtue of this, in today's world these words appear to have assumed a casualness in our discourse that diminishes, and blinds us from seeing, the explosive substance in their meaning.

The danger in over-familiarity with these concepts is that their significance in our lives can be compromised over the course of time. One may begin to accord them less attention than they deserve due to the way we, knowingly or unknowingly, have lessened or dismissed the importance of these concepts. We can diminish their importance by our indifference to, and lack of study of, the deeper meaning of these concepts. One can thereby begin to foster and live by a low-maintenance version and more convenient meaning of what destiny and purpose is all about. When we accord a convenient meaning to what purpose is all about, it means we reduce purpose to simply what we feel like doing with our lives. To the average human being, it is more convenient to spend our lives doing what is easy, what does not cost us much and what can be attained and achieve with as minimal hassle as possible. To do this and hinge our purpose on these yardsticks, we end up robbing ourselves and the generations to come. When we make purpose dependent on our feelings and whims, we end up only submitting to purpose just when we feel like it. We tend to do this when, as aforementioned, we do not walk with the right understanding of purpose in the first place. When we do not fully release ourselves to attaining purpose, we end up undermining or silencing the potential in us that is designed to manifest only when we yield ourselves wholly.

Purpose is not a feeling or emotion or even a specific place. It is more than that. It is the life assignment and calling God has ordained for you to execute on earth. Just as the question of your existence was not an afterthought, your destiny and God-given purpose was equally not an afterthought. It was sealed in Heaven above and you had no say in the conclusion.

A crucial step is to understand the truth that one's God-given purpose is the unseen architectural structure upon which and around which life is framed. In an ideal world, we will all happily accept this and skip into the destiny God has earmarked for each soul on earth. The reality is not always so. Sometimes the battle is first to discard the "it's-my- life" mentality that is sold to us by the present world we are in. It can be quite a struggle for some to tune into a higher paradigm that gives the concept of purpose its rightful place in our minds and hearts. This higher paradigm is centred on precisely the opposite of the it's-my- life mentality that is so commonplace in our world.

It is possible to find it difficult accepting that there is a plan for you that precedes you and is bigger than you. This difficulty usually stems from the reality that the issue of destiny is God's own decision and not ours. This usually does not sit well with many primarily because as humans we are wired to elevate freedom of agency and self-will above all else. We prefer to resort to, and operate in, that mode of complete freedom and self-will including on the matter of purpose. We tend to exalt the sense of freedom and self-will to priority status in our thinking and doing.

As a result, in our constant desire to exercise our free will, as humans, we may seek to also override or re-write what's been written by God for us. Along the way, the path into destiny is littered with various choices we have made, do make and are yet to make. The desire or disposition of seeking to interject God's plan with our own desires and decisions may manifest in the kind of choices we make along destiny's path. Our choices can either tell their own story of submission to God or submission to self. Which of the two we end up submitting to can heavily impact upon the journey we go through and where we eventually end up.

Crucially, destiny does not spring up on us the moment we mature to an age of accountability: destiny's clock ticks right from the moment our existence is sealed by God. This is even before we are conceived and eventually born on earth. It is as real as the reflection we see of ourselves when we look in the mirror. However, because destiny is not a physical construct that our senses can engage with, it is oftentimes neglected, dismissed or denied altogether. This notion that that which is invisible, unseen or intangible to our senses can afford to be neglected is a deception.

As crucial as oxygen is to life on earth it is unseen and oftentimes forgotten about in our daily breathing through each day. Divine purpose is oxygen for our spirit man and one cannot afford to neglect it. Jesus Christ breathes divine life into our spirit man. Divine purpose written by God is what sustains that enlivened spirit man to do what it was designed to do, which is to enliven. We are enlivened to be an instrument of enlivening. The means of enlivening is what differs from soul to soul and must be sought out by each soul.

Denial of one's destiny is ultimately to one's peril. If man can manufacture an inanimate product to meet a need or have a particular function for the benefit of a consumer, it is much the case with God, the Creator of all. The God of all wisdom and knowledge has an objective for placing you, a uniquely made being, on this earth. An imprint made in some sand can fade with time, but destiny is an imprint by God that does not fade with time. Though it may be fought, fled from, forgotten, it will never be erased.

In view of this, there is need to acknowledge that there is some assignment upon your life, seek to discover it and, when you do, embrace it. When there is a failure to discover your life's purpose one will easily fall into substitutes, second-bests or alternate life paths that look glossy and comfortable but they are not God's own, original plans for you. It is a possibility to miss God's original plan for our lives but it is never too late to re-route back to God and seek for Him to or-order one's steps to the end- point that He would have you get to.

Following these alternate routes may not navigate you to the specific and unique end-point which God's own designed route would have taken you to. Such substitutes can arise when we resort solely to our minds, head knowledge or voices around us to reign in the matter of our life pursuits.

Having an understanding of your purpose will allow you to pursue aright, sacrifice aright, and make the right decisions and choices that will characterise your life. The Lord Jesus Christ, when on earth in human flesh, acknowledged daily the imprint of destiny that was sealed in the heavens above that He should suffer death by crucifixion. As a result of this, He shunned every detracting thought, every detracting company and sacrificed maximally to ensure that this imprint of divine purpose was accomplished and not aborted (Matthew 16:23).

Having a recognition of what imprint God placed upon you from before you were even conceived will dictate your waking and sleeping thought, your actions and inactions, the people you choose to surround yourself with and other inexhaustible elements of how you spend your time on earth.

The life of the intentional, purpose-driven single must be underscored with a soul-deep awareness of who you are in God. The knowledge of who you are will be crucial to excelling in singlehood and optimises the quality of your life and service when eventually you come into a union with your spouse. If your spouse is a door and you are the handle of the door, but you are blind to the fact that you have been crafted as a handle, what you would have brought to the union is compromised because you have no bearing on your God-given identity. When there is a misalignment in purpose, as a result of ignorance of one's destiny, cracks can begin to form and crystallise. This results in lack of fulfilment and a marriage that morphs into a purpose-starved union.

The imprint of destiny is self-defeating if it is left as a mere imprint. The essence of the imprint is in its manifestation. In other words, the imprint of destiny finds its expression through a carrier. Creation of the carrier is a crucial part of bringing to fruition what the imprint of destiny holds. A transaction of creation therefore takes place in which God invests in the formation of a life with the expectation that the life created will engage with, submit to and remain committed to their discovered destiny.

The work of creation is God's first recorded work in the book of Genesis. God's ability to create and re-create is one of His defining attributes. In creating, God's life-giving power is exercised. God in His unfathomable counsel, omniscience and unsearchable wisdom had a finished picture of you before He started the process of forming you. This can be likened to what took place in Genesis' account of creation. God already saw the light before He called it into existence, partly because He is the Embodiment of light Himself. This is why God already knew beforehand what light looks like and what would happen when the light is introduced into the expanse of darkness that was the earth. The creation of light was not an exercise in trial and error, and neither was your formation.

The finished picture of you, from the detail of gender to nationality, the family environment you would be born into, to race, to genetic make-up, were intentional in God's design but secondary to the place of His purpose for your life. Your own unique mix of the aforementioned features are not designed to frustrate your life purpose, because God is not an author of confusion. God does not give you an assignment, only to deny you the very mental, physical or other resources you may need to execute it. Rather, a bespoke blend of features that make you unlike any other human under the sun, one way or the other, were designed to facilitate and help enable the execution of your purpose.

It is not the most palatable of experiences to be born into a poor household, but God may have seen that, for you, it will take growing up in such an environment to engineer into the fabric of your being a divine burden for the less privileged, for whom you have been raised as a deliverer. In other words, if God scours the whole earth and all the families of the earth and elects for you to come forth into the lineage of a specific family that may be struggling, imperfect or deficient in one way or the other, it is not a coincidence. If you therefore have hitherto hated your humble beginnings, despised the environment you may have grown up in, somehow you are despising a big part of your story that God himself allowed for a specific plan that all ties into your purpose.

Your creation is akin to a signature on the dotted line. Your existence is a commissioning contract signed by God in which the Source of your life declares that a particular imprint of destiny has been released to this particular soul for execution. All potential, as is found in God Himself, is placed in the invisible mass of cells that is the beginning of your creation. God oversees your creation curve throughout the formation stage and intervenes where He so wills. The hour of birth is a culmination of relentless working of the Heavens, fashioning, crafting, breathing upon, uprooting, altering to result in the coming forth of the life that was you. This however was just beginning on its journey. However, you may have come into this world, whatever your story, know that there is a reason, there is a cause, an intention behind your being present on earth. You may not understand it now in this moment, but you will in time come to discover that there is, and has always been, a divine intelligence at work in you.

* * *

Questions to Ponder

1. Have I understood that there Is an Imprint of destiny upon my life, Artist of which Is God?

2. Have I recognised that this Imprint must not be left dormant but Is there to be activated?

3. How can I engage with the purpose God has ordained for my life?

Scripture Corner

"... all... were created through him and for him." –

Colossians 1:16C (KJV)

Declaration: I recognise that there is a God-given purpose to my life. I resolve to seek to understand that purpose. I resolve to embrace it and run with it. I accept that living life without pursuing purpose is a disservice to myself, to my generation, my God and to my future spouse and our union...

-: CHAPTER 2 HIGHLIGHT: -

"A crucial step is to understand the truth that one's God-given purpose is the unseen architectural structure upon which and around which life is framed."

NOTES

3

THE TREASURE OF DISCOVERY

The word "discover" consists of the root components: 'dis-' and '-cover'. When one discovers, it is akin to removing the cover upon that which has hitherto been covered. That which has been discovered, is no longer covered nor hidden, it is now revealed. The process of discovery is itself a treasure as well as what the process eventually reveals. This is because the process of uncovering is a liberating, emancipatory process and oftentimes it is in the process that there is a becoming, a transitioning, an enlightening that takes one from one level of consciousness and awareness to another. In the process of searching, seeking and discovering, there is a fashioning that is at work in us. We find that in the process of discovery the level of our understanding ascends and the landscape of our thinking about who we are is transformed.

If for instance something you are searching for seems to be difficult to find, it can cause one to give up and to concede that thing. However, it can also cause one in many instances to begin to strive, push, determine, a-hunger for that said thing. By the end of all the pushing, striving, determining and persevering that takes place in the period of searching, we oftentimes end up coming out of the process with a greater depth of those mentioned qualities. The concentration, so to say, of perseverance or inner strength or determination in our inner man will be higher than it was at the start of the searching process.

If on the other hand we find that in the process of searching for a given thing, apathy takes over instead, it indicates to us that over time we have become less thirsty for that said thing. Either way whether we know it or not, we are changing for the better or for the worse through the process of searching for something. Fighting or campaigning for a given privilege, for instance, can oftentimes be the more exhilarating period than the period thereafter when that fought-for privilege becomes freely accessible.

This is especially so when that fighting or searching process is prolonged. When it comes to the concept of purpose, the discovery of it is its own awakening journey that every soul, especially the child of God, needs to undergo. Purpose is an indispensable treasure that needs to be brought down from the potential into the actual. This journey of knowing and fulfilling purpose begins through the process of discovery.

In life we see that no two stories are identical. As unique and custom-made as our fingerprints are, so are our stories. There may be some overlap between your human experience and your neighbour's. There may be some narratives, life trajectories, that align more than they differ, but no two stories, lives or destinies are identical duplicates. There will always be a differing detail, timeline, angle, target, reach or design that makes you to be your own original and the sole steward of your destiny. This is testament to the infinite and inexhaustible creative prowess in God: with the billions of souls that inhabit the earth, there is a specific destiny package that is distinctly crafted, each with a different name on it.

With this in mind, you have a responsibility to God, to yourself, your future spouse and to your generation to discover your purpose. In the supremacy of His counsel, God may choose to reveal ahead of time what your destiny is. In this instance, the revealing of purpose may not be preceded with prolonged seeking, as is seen in the lives of certain biblical characters.

Samuel as a tender infant did not appear to engage in prolonged seeking of God's face before his purpose was revealed to him, according to the biblical account.[11] On the other hand, another biblical character, Jacob had to seek till he prayed through to the revelation of his purpose. Jacob determined in his heart that he will not relent in his quest to be answered by God and elected to intensely not just seek, but to seek until there was a response. The keyword is 'until' which denotes a resolute, resilient resolve to find. He witnessed the fruit of this and experienced the treasure of discovery when he prevailed with God (Genesis 32:26). The experiences of these two personalities illustrate the diversity of operations of the Spirit of God and the differences in the route into destiny: one tirelessly sought and wrestled to obtain an answer whilst the other did not appear to do so to the same extent.

However, it is needful to see God's principles as the yardstick that one is to strive to abide by. God's principles always transcend individuals and personalities. Rather than solely resting our focus on God's relationship with certain biblical personalities, how He responded to them individually and letting that entirely define our approach to

---

1   1 Samuel Chapter 3

seeking God, there is need to also be moved by God's stated principles. One of such stated principles include the seeker principle.

The seeker principle is the principle of asking to receive, seeking to find, knocking to be opened unto. This seeker principle is an essential part of realising destiny and is the default principle that is operational. Whichever path God takes you on, the art and process of seeking God is as important as what one is seeking from Him. God esteems this discovery principle so highly that He continues to reinforce this principle in His Word. It is usually after He is sought, and that with all one's heart, that He, and that which we seek of Him, will be found of us.[22]

This process of discovery, seeking to uncover, should therefore be embarked upon early. The quicker you can get to know your purpose and see it with it your mind's eye, the earlier you can run with it. Sometimes, when we seek a given thing from God, whether that is information of some sort or impartation, it may come instantly or it may require some determined waiting.

In like manner, answers from the throne of God are titbits of treasures that may be so important that it may not be a casual affair getting those answers. Rather it most likely will entail tarrying in God's presence, showing sufficient desire to the Heavens above that you really ache to be furnished with the answers you seek, before God can entrust you with precious and strategic information. God etches out a glorious purpose, but it behoves us to stir ourselves into having a hunger, an enduring hunger, to grasp the fullness of that purpose. It may not simply fall into our laps without our own role being played.

---

2   This is seen in both the Old and New Testaments.

It is needful to stress at this stage that guesswork and assumptions based on logic and human reasoning will not suffice as a pointer to your God- given destiny. Whilst the process of discovering purpose will not ban any use of reason, it will not rely solely on human reason. This is because its origin, the origin of your purpose, is outside of and transcends human reasoning. In other words, it is not by your reasoning that you came to be. Your coming to be, and the reason for your coming to be, transcend you and the best of your logic and reasoning faculty. In other words, it is bigger than you and you will need to resort to that transcendent Authority who formed you to obtain details as to the 'why' behind your coming to be. It is noteworthy that being successful by the standard of the world, or your fellow man is not a yardstick or indication that one is walking in the purpose their Creator has designed for one.

A key digging tool for discovering the treasure of purpose is desire and a deep hunger. There must needs be a hunger in you both to embark on the process of discovery as well as a hunger to engage with what is discovered. Hunger being considered here speaks to the restlessness to graduate from generalities to the specifics of your life. The 'specifics' being referred to here encompasses information from God about you.

From where to reside to where you'll need to study to what friends to make to which way to turn at various junctions in your life, God can feed you with information pertaining to the unique road map of your purpose. Most people, if not all, seek to be successful. Most people, if not all, seek to leave a legacy for generations to come. But there is a step further to go and that is to grasp what that success means for you, based on the parameters of your destiny.

This further step will have an urgency attached to it when there is sufficient hunger in your heart to discover.

There is a temptation, even for Christian young adults, to latch onto an external construct of success which society seems to be wholesaling to the world. It may be that you have somehow bought into the success being sold to you by the world around you. If you observe that this is your circumstance, it simply shows that there is a vacuum in you which is currently being filled by what you are seeing around you and not what you are seeing within you.

It is imperative to therefore shift your attention from the outward to the inward and ultimately upward. The shift from outward to inward is necessary because hunger can only come from within you. No one can implant their own hunger inside you. No one can superimpose their hunger onto you else it will become another person's vision you'll be pursuing and sooner or later that external hunger will not be able to sustain you.

You need to have a paradigm shift within you that will generate a hunger. Pausing to shift your attention inward at least begins this process. This means putting the rat-race of each day on pause, reviewing where you are now in your life and re-examining what it is you are living for, striving for, aiming for and comparing that aim to the place of purpose. Are you living reactively, responding to what comes your way as your logic dictates or are you living proactively taking charge and living intentionally to align each passing day to your destiny?

Oftentimes, we are hungrier for what can be gained in the now at any expense. As humans we tend to pursue more energetically that which we can see and touch and feel in the immediate due to our constant desire for instant gratification. Purpose-pursuers are rather eager to ensure that they strive to leave their legacy intact by streamlining their living to not just casual living but to purpose-filled living. For a purpose-pursuer the here and now may not be that wonderful a picture they wish for but there is a recognition that the sacrifices of the present will pave the path for their future and in good time the gains that purpose brings will come to surpass the fleeting indulgences of the now.

After one has shifted their attention inward to examine whether there is the hunger in them to walk in divine purpose, there is need to then shift one's attention upward which entails communing with your Maker, seeking, observing and listening. As you resolve to discover your purpose, there is need to be resolute about it, just as Jacob was resolute about getting an answer from his encounter. You can alight from the bandwagon of living casually which you may have been on. You can alight from the bandwagon of trial and error for the bandwagon route is too costly to your destiny and to you. Resolve today to begin the journey of discovery and let it be a journey that results in an uncovering, an awakening and a new dawn in your life.

* * *

Questions to Ponder

1. Am I hungry for something in life? If I am, what Is that thing? If not, why Is this so? Questions to Ponder

2. How much have I discovered about the purpose for my existence and my divine destiny?

3. Have I started to seek God? If yes, am I a resolute seeker or have I become a tired ex-seeker of God?

Scripture Corner

"It is the glory of God to conceal a thing: but the honour of kings is to search out a matter." – Proverbs 25:2 (KJV)

Declaration: I make a decision to discover what I am on earth for. I submit myself to the process of seeking to uncover and seeking until the treasure of revelation is uncovered. I owe it to God, to myself, to my generation and legacy thereafter to realise the fullness of God's counsel for my life. But I cannot do this if I have not discovered what that counsel, what that package, what that purpose is.

-: CHAPTER 3 HIGHLIGHT: -

"There will always be a differing detail, timeline, angle, target, reach or design that makes you to be your own original and the sole steward of your destiny."

NOTES

SECTION 2

UNDERSTANDING SINGLEHOOD

4

THE GLORY OF THE YOUNG

As we navigate our way through life, from birth to the ensuing formative years, there is this curious chapter in one's earthly sojourn. It is titled Youth. Whether a teenager or an adolescent in the early stages of freshly- entered adulthood, it is a stage which cannot be bypassed. There is no shortcut that allows one to avoid this crucial stage, yet it is a phase of life that can leave one more confused than it met one, depending on how these years are used and spent. It can be a period of evolving, maturing and arising. It can equally be a period of faltering, stagnating and getting lost. In other words, destinies can either be manifested or can be marred during this strategic period.

It boils down to the use of an important but finite resource that is peculiar to the young. This resource is seen as what constitutes the glory of the young. That resource is strength, in its various forms. The Young have been given an inherent and divine capacity to accomplish, achieve, actualise and attain greatness, glorious feats and exploits, whether it be in the secular or the spiritual sphere. The mind of the young, more-so perhaps than other age-ranges, have a heightened capacity to imagine, envision, express creativity and manifest fearlessness due to a decreased regard for risk.

The young tend to be fuelled by a passion and zest for life that is akin to the care-free all-possible mentality of a child who does not see in the dimension of limitations but in the dimension of no limitations. Young David of the Bible did not analyse the magnitude of the situation he was venturing into – going into a battleground with no armoury for protection in which he could have suffered serious physical harm.

For him, it was simple. He believed that God is all-powerful and he believed that the all-powerful God should not be disrespected, not on David's watch. With this mindset, unsaddled with the preoccupation of what could go wrong which experience and age oftentimes brings, he moved. This epitomises the approach of the young, excessive thinking is not a part of the machinery of the young.

In David's case, this ironically brought about a greater manifestation of strength. An onlooker may have judged David's exploit in facing a warrior, holding a weapon as lethal as a gun, with a mere stone as foolish, but this was not David's view. David's simplified assessment of the situation, combined with his faith in God was a powerful fusion. An older mind, however, as is seen in the response of David's elder brother, will naturally see through the lens of much knowledge, reason and experience. This lens usually esteems more highly what could possibly go wrong and puts more weight on that possibility of something going wrong. This power that is in many ways peculiar to the Youth is a huge weapon that one can wield to victory or wield to one's downfall, depending on the choices of that young person. The young David had fire in his belly to defeat the menacing giant named Goliath. Another menacing giant was Nebuchadnezzar whom young Daniel and the Hebrew youths were not cowed by, even when their life was on the line. They were passionate and had a hunger to defend their God.

This overtook caution, logic, reason and possibility of death. Whilst an older mind that is zealous for God can do the same feat as young Daniel, it takes less for the younger heart to decide than it would for the more elderly. Recognising that the glory of the young is their strength will make one not impose on a young person what their constitution cannot bear. Their strength is their glory and that strength can be difficult to contain because it is not designed to be contained. Strength, like pressure, must surely find a point of escape or release.

The Christian youth who has surrendered to Jesus must accept that their strength must be streamlined and sown aright for there to be a safe take- off of their destiny. For the young person, the strength being described encompasses one's ability, prowess, zest for life, willpower, vigour, stamina, gifting and several other elements that all come under the umbrella term of strength. This strength ultimately must find expression or release one way or another, it cannot be sat upon or suspended. It will find its way out in some shape or form. This is why it's oftentimes seen where this strength is not harnessed or channelled aright, it spurts out in a chaotic manner and is sown into that which does not profit.

Strength is a rod in the hand of the Christian young person and is an enabling resource for one's purpose. The reason for this is that the gains that can be achieved when one is in this physical vessel known as the human body is in some ways commensurate to one's level of strength. For the young person, there is an abounding strength that God has put in the youth which makes the physical vessel more capable and less inhibited than other age ranges. At this phase in a youth's life, ageing processes are yet to begin and ironically the lack of experience in the young means there is a tendency to explore and experiment, partly because of the unique fusion of an abundance of strength and an inherent mindset of being unstoppable.

Strength finds itself expressed in various colours: physical strength, mental strength, emotional strength, spiritual strength amongst others. There needs to be sufficient expression of each of these colours of strength for you to remain on the lane that connects you to your destiny. As well as this, it is needful to be sufficiently selective of what you submit each of these colours of strength to. Without sufficient expression and selective expenditure of your strength there is a possibility that the atmosphere that is conducive for the fruition of your destiny may not be generated.

With all the physical strength in the world, but zero mental strength, not much can be achieved. The mind is the engine house of the human vessel. Once a mind is broken, the physical body follows suit in quick succession. The ability to operate optimally as your purpose may demand is decreased, with all the spiritual strength in the world, but zero physical strength. Note that where this circumstance manifests, a paradox scenario emerges in which the young person has a wealth and great capacity of internal strength but it cannot find the optimal expression until all these aspects of strength are generated, even if it is to some partial measure. Until then such youth may likely manifest weakness outwardly even though strength sits within him or her, waiting to manifest.

Your strength can be streamlined to the shape of your destiny through godly precept, practice and the power of focus. Submitting to precept translates to submitting your strength to principle-based living, on a daily note. Principles give us the necessary rubrics, rules and restrictions that ensure that our God-given destiny is the chief consumer of our strength. These principles may be secular in the aspect of time-management, or spiritual in the matter of Biblical principles that pertain to godliness, righteousness and, of course, divine purpose. Being a student of precept, namely God's precepts, is essential to fulfilling one's God-given destiny. Leading a principle-less life is tantamount to allowing your days to be squandered to whatever appeals to you in the moment. A moment is enough, however, to disrupt and destabilise the pathway to fulfilment of purpose which has been laid out for you by God. It takes constant recourse to the Word of God, the Bible, to learn, reinforce and ever abide by the foundational principles that are instrumental in protecting that glorious strength in you for its rightful use.

Gaining mastery and discipline over the use of our strength is also achieved through practice of the aforementioned principle-led living. Practice relates to the application of destiny-enabling principles that find their power expressed when applied by the Christian youth. Practising a principle, for instance, about refraining from toxic friendships, will require the work of practising the art of saying the word "no", where necessary.

Without practice, the principle remains confined to the paper on which it is written. It remains stuck in theoretical head-knowledge and is not brought down into the heart, from where it can flow out from, into our actions and ultimately into our daily living. It is with practice that a principle becomes a mindset, a way of life, a lifestyle. Practice is as the flesh to the skeletal structure of principles that we learn of. This is the reason why a major profitable way of spending one's strength is in the zealous practice of Bible-based principles on a day-by-day basis.

The crown of this glorious strength in the youth is focus. Focus goes further than precept and practice in harnessing your strength because it acts as the arrowhead that guides that precept of God into activation in your life. When we remain in constant consciousness of the why behind our existence, when we are ever aware of our purpose, we begin to weigh all we do in the scale of God's plan for our lives. Focus keeps the picture of destiny etched in the fabric of your heart. When the vision and end goal is seen with the mind's eye, a propelling effect is created. Focus turbo- charges your strength and also makes you judicious of another resource in your hand, which is time – this shall be considered later in this book.

* * *

Questions to Ponder

1. What am I sowing my strength into? And why?

2. Am I applying the principles of precept, practice and focus to your strength? What principles guide my daily living? What Is the source of these principles?

3. How can I better apply Bible-based principles and increase my focus on purpose?

Scripture Corner

"The glory of young men is their strength..." – Proverbs 20:29 (KJV)

Declaration: I recognise that there is a strength inherent in me divinely implanted by God. I elect to be judicious about how I channel this strength lest it is squandered into that which will sap out purpose from my life. I determine to use this strategic phase in my life to immerse myself, my strength, my focus, my will into that which God has raised me for.

-: CHAPTER 4 HIGHLIGHT: -

"The Christian youth who has surrendered to Jesus must accept that their strength must be streamlined and sown aright for there to be a safe take-off of their destiny."

NOTES

5

THE NECESSITY OF INTERIM SINGLEHOOD

It is necessary for you to thrive as a single, in order for you to thrive as a spouse. To thrive as a single, you must undergo a period of singlehood and excel at it. You cannot thrive at something that you have not engaged in. Singlehood is the season in which the seeds of self-awareness, self-worth and service to your purpose begin to germinate, sprout and bear fruit. However, this season does not always bear fruit for anyone who is not intentional about being single. It is a crucial stage in life that is not to be dismissed, rushed, or spent in a constant state of lamentation. It is a time to be busy, productive and boldly single.

Being single is more than simply a time of awaiting marriage. To be single is not a deficiency of some kind or a pitiful state, it is a crucial part of your coming of age and is a period that is instrumental in the ripening of your destiny. Seeing singlehood as a lamentable state will hinder you from soaring as a single and thereby limit you from soaring as a spouse. Likewise, spending your singlehood pining in desperation after the next chapter of marriage will stop you from mapping out and maximising the present chapter of your life.

Whether marriage comes after the current phase of singlehood or not, it is its own bona fide, irreplaceable and crucial rung on the ladder of life. Adam, as a young man was required to spend a period alone in the Garden of Eden as the only human present with the animals, the plants and the presence of God. He was given authority, dominion and vision to labour on and pursue whilst at work in the Garden of Eden.

The giving of the work to him by God preceded his eventual marriage and was therefore a symbolism of the need to find one's "work" on earth in one's prime years as a single. If you are not chasing anything, when unmarried, you will be unfamiliar with the art of chasing. This will compromise your hunger and ability to chase purpose even after marriage. It is noteworthy that God is a progressive worker and the pursuit of purpose is never static.

In other words, marriage brings its own new dimension to your purpose and living out your God-given destiny continues and even advances further after one enters into marriage. The ten thousand that you and your spouse are designed to chase will be seriously compromised because of your inability or inexperience in pursuing, chasing and striving towards something in your single state. This means you will not be able to add your quota of pursuing, chasing, striving towards your marital vision even when you later become married.

The period of singlehood can be an eventful time and this may not always be in a positive sense. Sometimes singlehood is the ground to make the kind of mistakes that will be too costly if made in another stage of your life. If there is a chink in your armour, perhaps in the form of inferiority complex or a lack of focus, singlehood is the phase of maturing, of burrowing deep and having fundamental chinks seen to and worked upon. It is not ideal to neglect the necessary process of maturing that singlehood is designed to facilitate. We see all around us clues from nature that show us that most of the abundance all around us began from a single entity. The abundance of cells came from one fertilised egg. The abundance of generations of a lineage, when traced, will have come from a single person. The wholeness and wellness of the single determines the wholeness and wellness of the abundance that stems from that single entity.

There has to be a developed self in you first before you can have the power to help develop another person around you. We read of Deborah in the Bible and meet her as a wife, a prophetess, a judge, a mother. In other words, we see her in the full swing of her purpose having reached her ministerial Jerusalem, so to say. We do not get insight into her years as a young single lady trying to tread the path of life and discover her calling. However, from the fruit seen upon her life, it is clear that she was a purposeful single for that phase in her life in order to effectively transition into the mother in Israel that we eventually read of.

To arise for her land, she first needed to arise for purpose and tow the path of sacrifice in her single years. There are experiences during this phase that are meant to cause you to arise in knowledge, in wisdom and in understanding. If you fail to adequately arise aright you will be unable to feed that knowledge to your home and wider generation when the hour comes. The implication of this is that you, your home and the destinies entrusted to you help facilitate will be starved of information Heaven designed for you to release. In other words when you are not intentional about finding your position and purpose in God you will cost not just yourself but your generation.

If wisdom is a stranger to you in your single years and there is no impetus to reach a certain depth in God, especially in the single years that lack of depth will speak contrarily in the day when you are wishing to build a home. It is no wonder that years sown to ignorance and vain endeavours will not just be at one's expense but at the expense of one's future home (Hosea 4:6).

Singlehood is the period to latch onto your discovered purpose with full unbridled force and gain the spiritual, physical, mental and emotional stamina that will arm you for exploits both in the singlehood phase and the phase(s) thereafter. It is not a coincidence that it is seen as a stage that is described as a "coming of age". This phrase does not solely relate to the outward, physical changes that occur in a young man or woman, it is also supposed to also refer to the mind. It is God's design that there is a mental and spiritual coming of age in which there is an awakening to who one is in God and an arising to the fullness of one's purpose. This is not done overnight, rather, it is a journey which is best started and explored in the unmarried phase when one's self-identity is still being learned and understood.

Visions, goals and dreams are being birthed and weaned from the level of imagining them for the future to a level of making them fully-fledged pursuits of your present. Whether it be academic, spiritual, professional, financial or otherwise, it is a period of activity and not dormancy where there is motion designed to advance the God-given assignment upon your life. Having said this, the abundance of activity and the abundance of motion does not always equate to progress. Sometimes before we rush to run, there must first be a knowing of where one is running to. Singlehood is a time of knowing for oneself, one's worth and instrumentality to God so that one's confidence and assurance of ministry does not rest in friends' talk or random permutations but on information from Heaven's table, a table which you would have grown accustomed to hearing from over the course of your single years.

In this phase, as well as a gaining, there must needs be a shedding. As well as a retaining, there must also be a releasing. As we increase in virtue, awareness of purpose, preparedness of our vessel and other ingredients for a purposeful singlehood, there is also need for a shedding of attitudes, mentality and certain kinds of relationships in order to be effectively poised for this strategic stage of life. In other words, a young child will adhere to childish ways and this will be seen as in order, but as he matures there must needs be a shedding and departure from those childish ways in order for the way of maturity to take root in one.

This shedding can occur through the in-working of God in our inner man in different ways. It is through the intermittent and sequential shedding and gaining that the girl morphs into a maiden after God's heart and the little boy becomes a young lad after God's heart. God oftentimes describes Himself as a Refiner and oftentimes to refine a piece of metal there may be need to burn, chip away at the metal until it is sufficiently refined for the purpose it must serve.

It is noteworthy that it is not at the point of usage that the refining takes place, it must needs be at the stage of preparation for usage. No vessel is better than its level of preparation. In other words, a vessel cannot be used for more than what it has been prepared for. The timeframe for this process varies for each individual and is not only confined to singlehood but the process must at least begin and set in before one ventures into the world of matrimony.

Shedding is a process that can be seen in nature around us. We see this in plants and animals. We see that in the flourishing of life, shedding is never absent. Whether it is the outer layer of a seed burrowed in the soil or the outer skin on a human, shedding seems an inevitable, almost crucial, aspect of life on earth. In like manner, singlehood as a young lady or as a young man, without going through some form of shedding in some shape or form, is a singlehood that is not truly complete.

You cannot give yourself to someone when you have not first found, discovered and known yourself and what God has put within you. Doing so will make you rely on those around you to fill the space in your life that only purpose can fill. This is oftentimes too big a role for someone around you to play especially when that person is equally striving to pursue their own God- given purpose. The relative space and freedom one experiences during the stage of singlehood should be seen as a resource to be maximised and used effectively to ensure the next chapter of your life is not spent trying to compensate for a non-intentionally lived singlehood.

There will surely come an hour of manifestation when your God, future home and generation will all count on you to deliver. The misfortune is when you find yourself in the time you are supposed to deliver but you have not discovered what you are supposed to be delivering. We only get one shot at life on earth and each phase of our living including singlehood cannot be rewound. Let your singlehood period be a period of all-round personal development in the spiritual, mental, academic and other areas. Let your singlehood be a period of building on the treasure of discovery and delving into the well of your destiny.

* * *

Questions to Ponder

1. What has been my approach to singlehood? Have I been Itching for what's next or running with purpose in the now?

2. What are the things that need to be shed off during this phase?

3. What Is hindering me from moving Into the next level of growth for my life?

Scripture Corner

"... if therefore thine eye be single, thy whole body shall be full of light."

— Matthew 6:22B (KJV)

Declaration: My single years are intentionally given to me by God not to spend mourning and lamenting but thriving and arising. I decide to invest my single years into growing into the kind of young maiden, the young lad, God has planned for me to be. I see that I cannot rewind these years and so I determine to see singlehood as the platform to attain and even surpass the symbolic one thousand that I know, with God's help, I can surely attain.

-: CHAPTER 5 HIGHLIGHT: -

"Singlehood is the period to latch onto your discovered purpose with full unbridled force and gain the spiritual, physical, mental and emotional stamina that will arm you for exploits both in the singlehood phase and the phase(s) thereafter."

NOTES

SECTION 3

MAXIMIZING SINGLEHOOD

6

WRITE THE VISION: READ & RUN

It is one thing to know what your God-given purpose is, it is another to go beyond the level of knowing it to the level of seeing it. A key mechanism that takes purpose from a level of knowing it to a level of seeing it is writing it out. We see it when we lift purpose out of the mind, where it stays in thought form, and have it penned down, where it is articulated and expressed in written form.

In other words, to know your purpose or calling in your heart means that you see it with your mind's eye. To articulate your purpose in written form is a step further that serves to consolidate what your mind's eye has already seen by introducing it to your physical eye. To know a given thing in your heart uses its own set of faculties in the mind. To write out that same given thing employs a whole new set of faculties in your senses. The more you bombard your being, senses and immediate environment with what you are on earth for, the more you can engage with it.

Most, if not all major corporations do not just know their terms and conditions, they document those terms and conditions. This is oftentimes done in comprehensive detail. It is not commonplace for such organisations to assert that solely the knowledge of their vision suffices to the extent of defeating the need to write it out. In actual fact, in many instances they task themselves with documenting their objectives or goals due to the understanding that it is insufficient to simply know it. The success of their corporation depends on having a thoroughly set out position on key areas which is written out in a professional manner. In many instances, it is in writing it out that the vision becomes more structured and clear and as one writes out a thing one is forced to find a way to articulate it and not just rely on a knowing alone.

Certain industries attach weight to something only when it is in writing. If, for instance, an agreement is in spoken form, it may not carry equal standing in a court of law as a written, signed and dated document. It is perceived, to some extent at least, that there is an added layer of intentionality when one puts pen to paper to record any verbal agreement made. This is made clearer when the root of the word "write" is explored. From Middle English, the root word is "writen", and, from Old English the root is "wrītan" which means "to incise, engrave or draw". The term "engrave" implies something is set in stone, a word has been carved out into becoming an entity of its own that is now beyond you. It transcends, and is no longer relegated to, that little box in your mind where your vision may have been hitherto confined to.

It is noteworthy that wherever we see longevity, wherever we see legacy, wherever we see an enduring of a given thing or name or feat or exploit through the ages, there will be a written witness. There will be something that has been written down for the ages to come to witness and learn of. The visions of the patriarchs of the Christian faith were written down and passed down the ages unto us. God, in His Word, has a manner of instructing His prophets to write visions down.

During these days of old, writing what God said also served to introduce an added layer of clarity. The prophet would write out God's words as He instructed through His Spirit, which would leave minimal room for error, or the wrong information being passed unto the people. Clarity of vision is a crucial component in living purposefully as a young Christian. For where there is blurred vision, there is a blurred understanding of what it is you are assigned by God to do. A blurred understanding is fruitless in its work. Rather than enabling one to gain insight as to their destination point, a blurred understanding serves as a disabling force that weakens the strength of your grip on what you're pursuing.

From Moses to Isaiah to Jeremiah across the books of the Bible, God's approach when it comes to commissioning assignments to His servants

hallows the place of reading the vision, perhaps more so than knowing the vision alone. Whether it is the commandments written in stone or writing His judgement on a wall, God demonstrates that He is a Writer who used writing down as an instructive and strategic tool throughout the Scriptures. Had the series of inspirations, encounters, revelations that comprises the Bible remained unwritten experiences and did not translate to penned down passages of Scripture, generations would have been starved of the Word of God and the Life therein.

God Himself is a writer who taught His people of old to inculcate the tradition and practice of setting down information given from above in a form that will endure through time, which is the written form. The premium that God puts on the act of recording through writing is further seen in His possession of many Books in the heavens above where names, events and plans are all recorded.

Writing down, or recording in some form, your God-given purpose, goal or vision means less of your mind's capacity is consumed with storing it all. Leaving the vision stored in our minds alone can make it susceptible to being less clear to us over time. The picture that was once very defined can, in the course of time, become blurry. Words that may have made sense when they were transmitted or revealed to you by God through his Spirit can begin to lose their intensity or details can become fuzzy when we have only the mind to keep record of such a treasure as our revealed purpose. Let your revealed purpose not become a mere memory, a faded consciousness or a treasure you only engage with every now and then. It should be as real and alive to you as your name. When someone calls your name you identify immediately with the name being called, so it ought to be with your purpose.

Sometimes, God reveals in stages and He leaves dots which He would want us to connect. It will prove a herculean task to recall each detail without pouring out what He has made you to know in written form of some kind. When you write, you unconsciously attach a gravity. This is partly because in the process of going from a thought to a written sentence or paragraph the mind has ruminated over the thought, affirmed that thought and writing works to reinforce that thought. The mind reproduces that same thought in a manner that makes written sense.

Note that the eye is a key sensory pathway into your mind and heart. Feeding your eyes with what God has said equates to feeding your heart with God's mind towards you. This strengthens your endurance and output over the long run due to your mind experiencing renewal on a constant note. The experiences of today will be distant memories of tomorrow. Immortalise that treasure chest of divine experiences and discoveries that you encounter on the track of destiny. You can begin today by writing the vision, your vision. Let your eyes read it continually and cause you to run.

***

Questions to Ponder

1. Have I recognised the need to write my revealed purpose down?

2. Is there a place where I can articulate the precious treasure of God's calling upon my life?

3. Has the picture of my purpose that was once clear become distorted? If so, how can I correct this?

Scripture Corner

"... Write the vision, and make it plain upon the tables, that he may run

that readeth it." — Habbakkuk 2:2 (KJV)

Declaration: I decide today to spend some time channelling the thoughts and images in my heart of my calling into a sentence, a paragraph that I can see and run with. I see that the more I confront my senses with the reason God created me, the more fruitful in Christ I can become. I elect to not just be s carried of purpose but also a seer and articulator of purpose.

-: CHAPTER 6 HIGHLIGHT: -

"The premium that God puts on the act of recording through writing is further seen in His possession of many Books in the heavens above where names, events and plans are all recorded."

NOTES

7

THE UNSEEN SEED, THE SEEN FRUIT

Growth can be somewhat of a mystery. Once you were that little child looking up at the world. Your bones within stretched and unseen cells multiplied. These hidden processes had to take place before your outward being then grew. Now, with the passage of time, you may have matured and now the world is on eye level. Growth as a process is not usually a loud noisy affair that announces itself, neither does each cell inform one it is about to multiply and expand. Growth, as critical a process it is, is silent and remains silent as its work is done inwardly and eventually manifests outwardly. With the right input into the body, growth, though silent, is a sure and steady process.

As we tow the path of purpose, it is needful to recognise that growth must start off internally before the outward fruit is seen. The internal growth is hidden and far away from the naked human eye, but the eventual outward fruit is beheld by all, when the unseen aspects have been set in motion and gone their full course. It is needful to recognise that as physical growth takes time, so does the growth of internal, mental and other aspects of our being. Reaching the optimum level of operation and manifestation in our God-given purpose cannot be reached overnight if growth is to have its perfect work and effect in one.

Imagine a seed. There is a whole fruit inside that seed waiting to be formed and released. But without that seed first being a seed and undergoing the necessary growth whilst a seed, there is no way that the fruit inside the seed can sprout forth. Note that the seed, in the interim period, is in the soil and is hidden in the earth, un-applauded and un-celebrated.[3] In that unseen, un- applauded state, the seed undergoes a breaking, a shedding, a metamorphosing, a becoming.

In the unseen phase, it is a period to undergo those necessary processes that culminate in the fruit eventually being seen. The outward fruit when it's brought forth, is then showcased and celebrated when the unseen seed has undergone its designated time of hidden, soil-deep transformation. To neglect this instrumental part that being an underground seed plays would mean putting the eventual manifesting of the fruit in jeopardy.

God's design is that there are seasons of life in which, just like that seed, we undergo a growth phase that requires us to be unseen and un- celebrated. This period can be seen as a form of incubation period. In this phase, our growth curve, whether it be in the spiritual, mental, academic or otherwise, is steep, depending on whether one has maximized that incubation period. During this period, God is shaping us, building us to such a state that we can handle that hour of manifestation when it comes.

Premature manifestation can lead to sub-optimal results that weaken the impact one would have had if the manifestation followed patient submission to the unseen stage. To live for something, you will need to die to some other things and that will require you undergoing a journey. The misfortune that has befallen many is that there arises a

---

[3] Zechariah 4:10

desperation to transform from a seed to a fruit overnight and seek to bypass, shun or fail to maximise the transitioning process.

Being 'unseen' in a practical sense does not mean one must travel to a forest somewhere but what it connotes is a period of ordinariness where there is no extra-ordinariness manifested in that season. It is an interim phase between the discovery of destiny and the manifestation of destiny. Many great personalities of consequence such as John the Baptist, Jesus Christ, Moses and many more, were unseen for seasons of their earthly calling before their eventual showing. However, it is a principle that is not just applicable to great men. It is a design of God.

If the seed was intelligible, it would probably see life in the soil as mundane, not thrilling or spectacular. That seed may see a fruit and strive to be as that fruit which can cause the seed to shun the seemingly quiet, uneventful period under the soil. The moment it rejects the God-given process it has to undergo of being unseen for a while, it will put the eventual manifestation of the fruit in jeopardy. If, instead, the seed were to understand that it must undergo this phase in order for the fruit within it to yield, and that beautifully, it will happily submit itself to the breaking, shedding, metamorphosing and becoming that is taking place prior to its fruit manifesting.

God has all the power in the world to create instantly, but He demonstrates that He puts great premium on the concept of process. God could have created all humans in a grown state, like Adam, but He chose to put the man in a cell unseen to the human eye for the man to emerge after the process of time. In a world where there is a craving to be seen to do, to be seen to shine, to be seen to be something, God seeks a heart that craves to be unseen until and unless the time of showing arrives when God Himself will orchestrate one's manifestation.

Therefore, do not despise your period of little beginnings, of being unknown; rather treasure it. As big as your dreams are, they can only be as big as how much you submit to the process of God. As eager as you may be

for your glory and your God-given purpose to erupt, let there be a recognition that there is a price to pay of being unknown first in order to be eventually known and that on a successful note. Do not loathe the season of being unheard and un-celebrated. Do not detest being a spectator for a period and not a player on the field. It is a needful part of your process. Accept it and submit to all that the unseen period gives birth to in your life.

We live in an age where there is a seeking, a quest to be liked, to attract people to ourselves and what we believe we may have to offer to them. The common effect of this is a scrambling and struggling to form an audience, a followership based on our beliefs of what is in us. Whilst this is a popular approach, it is needful to note that nature itself teaches us the design of God but oftentimes nature's message is lost. When a seed undergoes its thorough work and comes out in the open as a fruit, the fruit itself still needs time to ripen.

Once it is ripe, the fruit does not need to beg people to reach out for it. The fruit will not need to solicit for attention or for an audience to pluck it from its place. Rather, passers-by will look upon that lovely fruit and be attracted to that ripe, juicy, mango or apple or whatsoever other fruit it might be. In other words, it will be the people gravitating to the fruit due to its sweetness. It is therefore better to focus more on being as ripe as one can be than on hastening into the manifestation phase. It is better to build and boil up the glory inside you to the point where your light is sought as a beacon in a world filled with darkness. Jesus did not need to announce His glory by scrambling for men's applause and attention. All He needed to do was to tow the path of devotion to His Caller (the Father) and His calling. The works He did, as He manifested what God had put in Him at the right time, spoke for themselves. At times, He would rather ask for people to not talk about what wondrous works He did but the magnitude of His purpose and destiny could not be hid or confined and one way or the other men flocked to witness the brightness of His rising.[4]

It could be that your period of being unseen coincides with a particular stage of your present studies and you are hidden away under a mountain of books you need to get through. When the hour comes, those efforts put in in the secret will later speak in the open. Simply submit to being that diligent, patient and purpose-driven seed.

Spiritually, it could be that God takes you through a period of intense sowing of the Word and ploughing the heart soil with the spiritual fertiliser that will be the foundation of your 'fruit' season. Surrender to whatever God passes you through. It will surely yield the eventual sprouting forth of that beautiful fruit called Destiny. Note that the more we sow into the unseen phase, the more we reap in the seen phase. Therefore, trust His path and His timing, not yours.

---

4   Matthew 5:15

* * *

Questions to Ponder

1. Do I feel a desperation to be seen by the world?

2. Am I ready to tread the path of God's timing and will for the hour of my manifestation?

3. How am I maximising my incubation period?

Scripture Corner

"And the child grew, and waxed strong in spirit, and was in the deserts till he day of his shewing unto Israel."

– Luke 1:80 (KJV)

Declaration: I submit to God's wholesome counsel for my existence. I see the trends around me and the pressure upon me to hasten into the limelight at whatever cost. I elect to dig deep to understand the building process God would have me undergo. I surrender to being the unseen seed that will ultimately sprout forth as that magnificent fruit when time, process and growth has had its perfect effect in me.

-: CHAPTER 7 HIGHLIGHT: -

"It is better to build and boil up the glory inside you to the point where your light is sought as a beacon in a world filled with darkness."

NOTES

8

SINGLE AND SATURATED WITH GOD

As a Christian single, you are in a crucial junction in your life. At this point, you have already clocked up a number of life-miles from your birth to this stage of adolescence and early adulthood. However, the distance that you are yet to travel, if Christ tarries, is far greater. Before you lies a host of unknown experiences, challenges, joys, difficult moments, successes and tribulations. Out there somewhere in the untravelled road ahead of you, you will meet many bus stops put in place by God. These bus stops may include academic milestones, marriage, milestones in career, parenthood, exploits in ministry and much more. These 'stops' are all contained in the destiny package that God has designed for you. To carry you through such journey of life, there is need to be saturated with God.

Consider the idea of travelling to a place you have never known of, or been to, before. Imagine making this journey with no assistance whatsoever from passers-by or from any GPS device whatsoever. You can be sure that there will be some challenges in the course of trying to make that journey on the mere basis that you have not travelled that path before. It could be that you may end up in the wrong place, or that it takes you thrice the duration it should have taken or you end up covering the distance of three times the actual journey. The reason is because there will have been all manner of wandering, misdirection and re-tracing of steps along the way. In this scenario, you are saturated with something: ignorance and confusion.

On the other hand, let's consider that you do attempt to travel to the unknown place, but this time with GPS that has clear signal. You will quickly notice glaring differences in the aspect of journey time, accuracy in making the right turnings and ultimately arrival at the right destination. The GPS can even inform you that you are about to go up a hill or pass a bridge or that there is oncoming traffic. It is noteworthy that in these two instances the destination is the same but the means of getting there is severely impeded in one instance, whilst in the latter instance the means of getting to that ultimate destination is made to be much more effective and fruitful.

As a single with yet many unknown twists and turns ahead of you, there is need to be connected to your GPS - God. The ultimate GPS one can have in one's life is one's creator - God. You do not know the terrain of what lies ahead of you but your GPS does. Your God does. The more of Him that fills your life, the more direction and meaning your life will have. You cannot be saturated with what you do not know. If you are to be filled to the point of saturation with God, you will first need to know that God, and that on an intimate and experiential level. God has to be real to you: not an afar Being you reach out to once in a while.

Remember that God is the sole custodian of your existence and is the only One who knows all that your existence will contain through this earthly sojourn. As a result of this, your life purpose is therefore in God. You cannot then expect to find your life's assignment outside of the One who has authored it. Note that replacing your purpose with some comfortable alternative or substitute, will not land you at the same destination point that your Maker- assigned purpose will.

Surrendering to God means that you submit to the Lordship of Jesus Christ over your life. Following true repentance from sin, you accept and believe by faith in the saving and redemptive work of Jesus Christ on the Cross of Calvary. You can then begin to build upon this foundation and begin ploughing the path of seeking God. Seeking God entails communing with Him through prayer and through His Word continually. It means a- hungering to know Him deeper and deeper with each passing day. It means walking closely with the Holy Spirit, our Teacher. With seeking Him there arises an urgent thirst, deep within, to experience His presence, His nearness, His glory and His power. Seeking is also the vehicle that takes one into the realm of hearing from God, knowing when God is speaking and when He is not.

This whole process cannot be effectively undergone alongside an entanglement with what God does not approve of. It is self-defeating if one hand is raised in worship and the other is clasping onto the world. In this sense, separation from what is not approved of in God's Word is required. Further to this, God can take one on a path of deeper consecration in which there is a higher standard of consecration He has designed for one and expects one to live up to.

This is especially so when there is a depth of experience that God would wish to pass you through to prepare you for what He has in store for you. All of this will entail some key sacrifices of your time, your energy, your own will, your commitment amongst other sacrifices. All these avenues of surrendering, seeking, separating and sacrificing work together to build up your God-saturation content. You can elect to tread the path of being saturated with God. As you do, your manifestation will be the better for it.

* * *

Questions to Ponder

1. Do I have a hunger for God?

2. What are the hindrances preventing me from delving deeper Into God?

3. Do I see a need to be filled to the point of saturation with God?

Scripture Corner

"And ye shall seek me and find me, when you search for me with all your heart."

– Jeremiah 29:13 (KJV)

Declaration: As a Christian single, I elect to be saturated with God. I acknowledge that God is my Maker, the Author of my Purpose and my GPS. I choose to be a seeker and finder of God. I elect a path of real closeness and intimacy with God. As I do, I know that everything else will fall in line.

-: CHAPTER 8 HIGHLIGHT:-

"It is self-defeating if one hand is raised in worship and the other is clasping onto the world."

NOTES

9

THE ARMOURY OF PLANNING

Oftentimes, we may wonder, imagine and hypothesise about what the future will hold. As humans we have a remarkable capability to envision and visualise in our mind's eye what has yet to take place. It is almost the brain's way of propelling us towards achieving some future goal or purpose. In our minds, we may find ourselves trying to picture some glorious destination in the future, whether it be the kind of home, achievements, job or the spiritual exploits one will have attained. However, there is need for more than solely envisioning what will be. There is a need for another dimension, which is where the armoury of planning comes in.

To plan is to go a step further from envisioning. When we only envision a thing and do not go further than this, we are confining that envisioned destination to our imagination alone. Our imagination may house lofty sights and great dreams, however there is a chance that such dreams may remain in this space as a mere fantasy and never come to fruition if we do not add the layer of planning. When we start to plan towards the envisioned dream, we no longer confine that envisioned sight to our imagination. Instead, by planning we begin to inadvertently promote and elevate that vision from a fantasy into a place in our reality. This then causes us to start to prepare and work towards it to ensure it is fulfilled.

The term 'armoury' refers to the place where weapons are usually kept and stored. To achieve any great feat, especially feats assigned by God to us, a number of tools need to be employed for a better chance at success. There are a lot of tools or weaponry we may have in our arsenal to achieve success in our God-given purpose, but any armoury where the weapon of planning is absent is not complete. Having a plan facilitates and orders the pathway to one's desired and destined end. Most great armies of the world, before deploying their resources for a particular mission, will have a plan of some kind that will order what steps shall be taken, why, by whom, when and how those steps shall be taken to achieve a specified aim or goal. In planning we translate this same theory into practice.

As mighty as missiles and nuclear weapons may be, what is more potent than thousands of missiles is a strategy, a plan, for how those powerful weapons are to be used. History, including biblical accounts, demonstrates that it is not an abundance of weapons that results in success, rather an abundance of wisdom. In this wise, wisdom swallows strength and in the same way purpose with a divinely-approved plan is greater than having purpose alone.

A plan enables one to break down what can look like a lofty dream into actionable elements. If, for instance, your revealed purpose is to conquer the nations for Christ through the sickle of a musical ministry, a plan may include daily or weekly practice routines to sharpen the sword in you. Diligence and commitment to destiny-enabling development plans allows one to remain on the right track that will usher the Youth into that glorious destiny. Having, and sticking to, a plan helps us to streamline the use of our energy output and to maintain a consciousness of who one is and why one is on earth - which we can sometimes lose sight of.

In committing ourselves to destiny-enabling development plans, we express total allegiance to, and faith in, what God has raised us for. We can only start planning for a given thing when that thing has become real to us, we are not in doubt of it and it is something that is significant to demand our strength, energy and focus.

It is noteworthy that we are crafted in the image of a God who does not only have a will concerning you, He turns that will into plans. For example, at the fall of man in the garden of Eden, God proclaimed that the seed of the woman would bruise the head of the serpent.[5] That was a purpose. God planned it such that all happenings between that point of declaration and Jesus dying on the cross would link up together towards the fulfilment of the plan and purpose of God declared ages ago. When we plan, we tap into that attribute and nature of our Maker. You can dream of greatness and you can equally plan for greatness. After discovering what you have been raised for, take time to also discover what actionable steps you need to take. Take time to discover your own part which God expects you to play to partner with Him in the fulfilment of your purpose. Consider, prayerfully, the practical steps that can connect you to that future YOU. Consider what practical aspects will best position you for that ministry. Consider the groundwork that may need to be put in towards honing the aspect of skill and gaining the requisite knowledge that pertains to your assigned craft and gifting.

---
5   Genesis 3:15

With respect to secular endeavours, you can plan for that career in your chosen industry by taking the necessary courses, gaining the necessary experience and acquiring the relevant credentials. All of these steps constitute a plan of some kind. God in-builds in us potential to advance and oftentimes provides us with the signposts to make us think and plan in the right manner. In whatsoever God would have you to do, there is a knowledge component and planning is needed to gain the necessary knowledge which is an important component of positioning yourself for what God has in store.

In the spiritual sphere, a personal consistent plan designed to make you delve deeper into God is key. Determine to reach into the future that God has for you by inculcating the right practices and discipline needed to develop your inner man. Whether it be gaining a deeper understanding of the Scriptures or building the peculiar prowess that God seeks to manifest in you, such virtue may not simply spring upon you spontaneously without diligently towing the path of self-development.

The best time to plan for a thing is before that same thing arises or occurs. The best time to plan for war is in the time of peace.[6] It is not beneficial to plan and prepare financially for a degree course after you have already started that degree. It is needful to assess before commencing the said course how it will be financed. In the same manner, we prepare and plan ahead for that envisioned dream in the now even whilst it may not have manifested fully yet.

Plan for your tomorrow today. That next phase that God is

---
6   Quote by Publius Flavius Vegetius Renatus.

making you understand is round the corner. What actions, steps, activities and developments are necessary now to equip you spiritually, intellectually, emotionally, financially and otherwise for that phase? Make your financial management plan whilst you are not quite in that expected wealth yet.

Plan how to reach the next level in the ministry God has called you into whilst you are yet in the current level where you are.

Start planning for that marital stage in your life whilst you are yet in your single phase. If you are persuaded that God is calling you into the vineyard of marriage, it is needful to not only pray to be the wife God has called you to be, but it is also needful to plan to be the wife God has ordained you to be. In addition to towing the path of prayer, plan practical steps to equip you with the understanding you need about what the institution of marriage entails. Take advantage of vetted, church-led and Christian- centric marriage seminars with a foundation in the undiluted Word of God. Examine and address erroneous notions of marriage you may have developed over the years. Plan to broaden your knowledge base as to what tools are required to build a home. Each day and each week can produce a better version of you than was present before.

As you elect to be a purpose-driven Christian, consider what practical steps in each sphere of your life that you may need to take advantage of in order to place you in the best state to receive, and grasp, the fullness of God's divine package for your life. As you do so, God will establish His will

* * *

Questions to Ponder

1. Have I recognised the need to be a good planner as well as a good dreamer?

2. What are the outstanding aspects of my purpose that I need to plan towards?

3. Am I ready to ensure I plan In God and not outside of Him and His counsel for my life?

Scripture Corner

"For which of you, intending to build a tower, sitteth not down first, and counteth the cost…" – Luke 14:28a

Declaration: I decide to elevate my vision, goal, dream and revealed purpose up from the place of imagination and fantasy into a place of reality through the means of destiny-enabling plans. I see that planning engages my mental, psychological and physical strength towards ensuring the fruition of my God-given destiny. I trust that as I plan with divine direction, guidance and revelation, the ground for the fulfilment I yearn for in the future will be laid.

-: CHAPTER 9 HIGHLIGHT: -

"Diligence and commitment to destiny-enabling development plans allows one to remain on the right track that will usher the Youth into that glorious destiny."

NOTES

10

SINGLES OF SUBSTANCE

Before considering who singles of substance are in the context of purpose, it is worth considering who they are not. In our day and age, it is popular to think that fulfilment is achieved primarily once one is married. Oftentimes, getting married is referred to as 'settling down'. Whilst this is mostly said innocently and no ill is usually meant, it does connote the idea that the unmarried are an unsettled, unstable breed who, in some ways at least, are to be pitied somehow. Such statements seem to suggest that, figuratively speaking, marriage can be seen as the full stop whereas singlehood can be seen as the comma, many would say. Some would go further to suggest that singlehood is a no man's land where one lives in a state of being fundamentally incomplete as a person and therefore remains unfulfilled.

When this approach is adopted by a young man or woman, there is a mournful, self-lamenting mindset that develops. One begins to bemoan one's unmarried state and covet marriage to the extent of seeking it at all costs. For such people, they may likely feel as though life is on pause when one is single. It can also be as though the volume dial of their existence is turned low. For them, marriage or a 'romantic' relationship of some kind is what validates them, puts life on play mode and makes their life to no longer be on mute. The implication of this is that for such people, marriage is what saves them from lack of fulfilment. Carriers of this mindset may likely do all they can to not remain single for long, as they genuinely believe that they are incomplete on their own. Such a mindset and thought is the antithesis of what singles of substance believe and stand for.

For singles of substance, marriage is not when life begins. Marriage is not the answer to any lack of fulfilment that one may be suffering. It will not suddenly kick start purposeful living. If one is unfulfilled, unsettled and not purpose-fuelled as a single, they may also be unfulfilled and purpose- starved as a married spouse. Furthermore, marriage does not make you complete, neither does one spouse complete the other. They are two people complete in Christ, whole entities joining together to multiply impact.

If a whole object is joined to a non-whole object, a chunk of the whole is subsumed in completing the other and the joint impact is therefore compromised. To know this principle - that to be successfully married requires one to be successfully single - is what differentiates singles of substance from others. To have too lofty expectations of marriage is to put too much of a burden on the institution of marriage and of course when a structure is overburdened it can buckle as it is being used beyond its designed purpose and capacity.

When an understanding of this aforementioned principle described above is active and operational in a young man or woman, they can be said to be a single of substance. Singles of substance are busy and their busyness is of the effective kind. The busyness of singles of substance is concentrated on living to cause impact and living for that which transcends them. For such a breed, for such specimen of singles, there is a consuming hunger that radiates from within to attain the extraordinary and ascend to the height that their potential demands.

Many in the full swing of singlehood have found themselves at various crossroad points at which a wrong turn may have been taken. With each decision that is taken and choice that is made, it can have a domino effect on other aspects and phases of our lives. Whether it is one's choice of friend, use of time or where one sets their focus, each decision has some direct or indirect impact on where we end up. Far too many people in our day and age, rather than going forth to conquer and be fruitful in purpose, have found that they themselves have been conquered. Many young singles have been derailed from the track of their life's destiny and found themselves at the mercy of chance and luck, living life by trial and error or at the behest of society and opinions around them. Many are rushing for and hasting towards what will come next and not focusing on what God has assigned them to execute in their 'now' phase.

From time immemorial there have been countless examples of young lads and maidens who have taken the bull by the horns purpose-wise and arisen in their generation. We find that such young minds did not have superhero powers or climb down from Heaven. Instead, they simply elected to tow the path of utter submission to their discovered purpose. By doing this, they became trailblazers and steered a quiet revolution in their world simply by being true to their divine and non-negotiable mandate from God. Whilst others sought to fit in, blend in and follow the norm, these singles of substance found the courage to do the opposite and strive to be the odd one out. In the process they arrived at fulfilment's door having ridden on the chariot of their God-given purpose.

The young man Joseph of the Bible was aware of the calling upon his life from his youth and recognised the need to protect and pursue that divine mandate given to him. Despite challenging circumstances that beset him roundabout, his steadfast submission to the vision and purpose revealed to him kept him focused and alert. He also recognised that to say yes to God's plan meant that he had to learn how to first say no. He had to say no to the compromise of his faith, to naysayers of his dreams and no to anything less than pursuing the fullness of God's plan for his life. In the prison where he was sent, he knew that, even though he may be imprisoned, his purpose was not. When sold to the merchants by his brothers, his life was being sold but the divine purpose for that life of his could never be sold to anyone or exchanged for anything.

Esther was a single of substance who recognised that achieving purposeful living requires adequate preparation. Esther was positioned as a separate and selected young lady on her way to somewhere unique. The realisation of this propelled her into another realm of thinking, planning and living. Her call to royalty was not written on her forehead but her decision not to join the bandwagon, her choice to pursue her ordained path despite her circumstances showed that the stuff she was made up of was not ordinary.

In an age when there is constant striving for popularity, applause and recognition, Esther proved that the path to the palace is not always the popular route, it is not always the well-trodden road. She was a queen not just from the day she was appointed but she was always a queen in God's sight. Every line in the story of her life was expertly written by God, every detail interwoven together to create a beautiful tapestry of His glory. In the hour of manifestation she stood, and did not stop, before the king and the glory which was radiating from within her spoke on her behalf and announced her presence.

Many Esthers of our current day have seen their crown dashed in pieces. Some crowns have been dashed by incessant distractions. Other crowns have been dashed by destructive dalliances that have derailed queens-in- waiting and kings-in-waiting from the divine path to their glorious future. In the process this has robbed them of the honour their purpose was meant to purchase for them. Others have sold their crown in exchange for approval from others, popularity or some other perceived gain. Having sold their crowns, their queenship or kingship is on the line, their purpose and the peace of all the generations that depend on or are linked to that purpose is also on the line. Perhaps it is time to pick up the pieces of the crown of purpose that has been tossed aside and find the way back to the palace of divine destiny.

Dinah was destined to be a single of substance but saw events in her life take a turn for the worse when she wandered. Eager to go and see what was going on in the land, she took herself away from the camp and walked into another part of the land – a new territory. She wandered from where her family had pitched into the surrounding environment where she intermingled with the people of the land. In like manner, for many singles, there is danger in straying. Straying can come in various forms. What was once held onto and pursued with all one's might can gradually start to be treated with less and less of the passion, focus and commitment it requires. This is also a form of straying.

At a point, purpose – and one's focus on it - can be dumped altogether and its position and place in our lives can become taken up either by someone or something else. The unfortunate truth is that, as is seen in the case of Dinah, one may not always be able to successfully retrieve one's steps back to the path of purpose unscathed. Even when one does try to later re- pursue that calling that they had dropped, compromised or traded, it usually comes at some kind of cost. That cost may affect the timing element of one's manifestation. It may also mean that emotional, mental and even physical wounds and bruises can be suffered by the single which following God's perfect path of purpose would have protected one from. Those wounds can oftentimes leave painful and lasting scars.

It is therefore for the young heart that is athirst for true fulfilment to arise into a singlehood of substance. It is time to no longer postpone the pursuit of purpose but to forsake the mentality of trial and error and step firmly into destiny's stairwell. Shake off the casual living and reach towards the new height that is found in divine purpose.

***

Questions to Ponder

1. What do I understand by the phrase Single of Substance?

2. What has my singlehood been centered on? How can I re-orientate myself to God's purpose for my life and emerge a single of substance by so doing?

Scripture Corner

"And beside this, giving all diligence, add to your faith virtue; and to virtue knowledge;"

— 2 Peter 1:5

Declaration: I decide to no longer desire to live the lives others are living. I elect to take hold of the life given to me by God and the purpose assigned to me and give my all to live for it. I may have been existing and going through the years cumbered with the stresses of life and consumed with the day to day demands that the bigger picture of why I am here has become blurry. I declare that I am a single of substance, driven by God's purpose for my life and on a mission to enter into the fullness of what Heaven has in store for my time on Earth.

-: CHAPTER 10 HIGHLIGHT: -

"Whilst others sought to fit in, blend in and follow the norm, these singles of substance found the courage to do the opposite and strive to be the odd one out."

NOTES

11

IN QUIETNESS AND CONFIDENCE

Life can be a rollercoaster of its ups and downs with various mountains and valleys which we have to navigate. The journey into the fulfilment of one's purpose is a path that exposes one to many experiences along the way. These experiences may be challenging and demanding at times. However, one way or the other God has planned for these experiences to be part of His process for you, part of your becoming and part of your own eventual manifestation.

It is needful to pay attention and be alert to the big picture that God reveals to you about that glorious destination He has ordained for you. It is also needful to pay attention to the step-by-step pathway He leads you along which will be an emancipatory pathway that lifts you from where you are now to where you need to be to enter the fullness of His divine package for you. This pathway is not an overnight experience and one key silent requirement is the need for quietness and confidence in God. This will keep impatience, seeking shortcuts and any trade-off of your destiny far away from your thoughts. This specific phase in your life, in which you are a single young adult striving to live purposefully, will have its peculiar pressures. Living purposefully can oftentimes mean going against the grain, standing out from the crowd, stepping outside the box of conformity. This can, and does, take you to a lonely space where not many voices around you are speaking the same language of purpose.

Living purposefully will mean making necessary but difficult choices and mastering the art of saying 'no' where needful. This enables one to guard and protect the purpose and potential that resides inside one and also guard one's capacity to attain that purpose and potential. As a young person, the instinct to wish to belong, fit in, be popular may need to be pushed against and eventually overcome. This is so that you have the mental capability to approach each pressure or pitfall from a place of what God has told you and not what human voices have told you.

So even when it looks like the road is bumpier at certain junctions and it may appear that the horizon seems somewhat blurry, focus on playing your role and remain steadfast in the path of God's plan for your life. It won't be long before you look up and see that the envisioned horizon has not only become clear, but it is also no longer afar off. It is now within your reach.

Where you are now in this specific period in your life, as well as all the other phases in your life (past, present or future) cannot be rehearsed; neither can it be rewound, re-lived, fast-forwarded or lived in slow motion. We only have one shot at being here on earth, only one shot at being young and only one shot at pursuing the God-given purpose He has crafted for our lives on this side of eternity.

This one shot can easily be squandered away and spent as wasted years culminating in no remembrance of you or your time on earth. On the other hand, this one shot can be a junction in your generation that will bring colossal impact for good unto your world whilst you are alive, and through your legacy thereafter. The one-shot mentality when imbibed will propel us to strive with all that is within to immerse ourselves in the pursuit and execution of God's unique purpose for one's life.

A common circumstance that can easily arise in life is when fear find its way into our path, into our lives and takes root therein. There are so many unknowns, twists and turns to life and sometimes that in itself is enough to make us hasty, seek for shortcuts or forsake the path of God's purpose entirely. We may hurriedly trade what seems to be a faraway future fantasy with what our hands can easily grasp in the now. But despite the noises that may surround you, noises from your mind speaking fear or perhaps from voices around you, there can arise a quietness and confidence within you that fills your life and gives you strength through it all to remain purpose- focused.

You may likely see others living out their God-given assignments. Some of them may be your colleagues and loved ones. You will witness other people's purpose being played out and you will likewise come to hear of their triumphs. But what everyone may not shout about are the toils that paved the track of triumph. You may not witness the personal cost behind many of the celebrations you come to witness in the lives of those around you.

Seek not another person's trophy, be content to be your own original and labour for your own. Times may arise when your present circumstances seem not to sing the same tune that God is showing you in your dreams. Moments of disappointment can litter the path to success. Yet let your heart ever lean upon and trust in God's process. As you trust, you become quiet within and confidence in God's plan and timing arises.

Quietness, in the biblical context, denotes peace, stillness. It may sound like an irony but quietness is a roaring symbol of strength. Quietness carries something that the tumult lacks which is calm. Where there is calmness, there goes a conqueror. You may have been crippled with self-doubt and confusion, re-trace your steps to ascertain where you may have lost your way. Tune your heart back to the Author of your Existence and His promises for you. In Him, trust. As you do, you will no longer be enslaved by the dictates of your senses. Rather you will operate from a place of assuredness in God and will feel sufficiently secure and steadied having anchored in the knowledge that you have a constant Companion on this path of destiny.

Once this assuredness is operational in one, you will no longer see a tendency to be in a race with life, to compete with the person beside you as to who must be the first to attain some blessing. For all that will do is make you live your life in second-best, catching-up mode. Your sights may be set on not being left behind but all that does is keep you looking in the wrong direction. When stripped of its packaging and the eloquent explanation you may have of why you live this way, the root cause is essentially a severe lack of divine quietness and confidence within.

This lack is several-fold. It could be lack of confidence in the God who has raised you and in what God has put inside you. God is an Author that writes only perfect lines. When He authors a project, that project will have a mastery about it that will testify that it has God's seal and fingerprint. We as humans cannot think up a better plot to our existence more than the One who crafted our existence. Unfortunately, where we try to outwit God by seeking to do our own thing and toss aside the purpose He has for us, we merely serve to outwit our own selves and jettison true peace and fulfilment.

Right where you are, you can see that all around you there is a wonder about nature around us that tells a story of a glorious God with glorious power. Animals and plants rely on Him to take them through each passing day and provide all they need to survive. Unfortunately, humans in our superior mental capacity seem not to. However, we can elect to entrust the Artist of the Universe with our lives and future. As we do so we facilitate our own becoming, our own arising, and our own manifesting that posterity will be grateful for.

***

Questions to Ponder

1. Do I feel a contentment and peace to await God's timing?

2. Are there heights I am aiming to achieve? Has an impatience or frustration crept into my heart and taken root?

3. What concrete steps will I take to reconnect to the strength that is in quietness and confidence?

Scripture Corner

"In quietness and confidence shall be strength;"

– Isaiah 30:15

Declaration: I see the treasure of quietness and confidence in God. I will ever strive to guard my heart from tumult around me and actively determine to put all faith and assurance in God's perfect ability and timing. I declare that I am God's project and pleasure and I know He is crafting a glorious manifestation of divine purpose in my life. I will seek to tap into the strength that comes from the quietness and confidence in Him.

-: CHAPTER 11 HIGHLIGHT: -

"Whilst others sought to fit in, blend in and follow the norm, these singles of substance found the courage to do the opposite and strive to be the odd one out."

NOTES

SECTION 4

THE NEXT PHASE TO CONSIDER

12

FROM SINGLE TO SPOUSE

It is needful to note that life as a single, for many, will be a phase that will potentially give way to another chapter in one's life - marriage. This new chapter of marriage will be a relatively more lasting stage in one's life and will contrast the relative transience of singlehood. Whilst there are many that may wish not to tread the path of matrimony, there are yet many that do. For the latter category of young singles, there must needs be an effective transition from life as a purposeful single to a fulfilled and vision- chasing life partner when the time comes.

Failure to transition effectively can cause one to see marriage through the same lens with which one viewed singlehood. When this happens, the distinction between the two phases and peculiarities that are unique to each of the two phases will be overlooked or dismissed, causing a distorted perception of marriage to arise in the mind.

Living as a fulfilled single necessitates a can-do mindset that is not constrained by the need to align with one's spouse's demands or desires. There is a freedom and sense of entitlement that permeates the single's thinking and life. This affords one the ability to think, plan and act as one pleases. With this, comes a strong sense of independence, reliance on self and pursuit of purpose on one's own terms. In other words, it is normal to get so immersed in a lifestyle that exalts self-reliance and independence in one's single years. However, it is needful for one to adequately re-calibrate one's mind to the new landscape that marriage demands and requires.

The single years are best spent with the aforementioned sense of endeavour, striving to live as a go-getter and maximising the period of being, to a considerable extent, your own boss. However, for a seamless transition into the next chapter, there must needs be a reconciling with the reality that one's sense of control may change as one moves on from singlehood into marriage. On a human level, marriage can be a strange and new territory for many that are not used to doing life with another human being.

Holding on to the single life whilst trying to fit in marriage around it will not work. This is why a de-briefing phase where one studies to prepare for single-less living is in order. Many have entered into the next phase and become frustrated, disappointed or unfulfilled due to applying the round peg of pre-marital lifestyle to the square hole of the lifestyle of the married. The Christian model of marriage is based on submission and the husband being the head of the home. It is not the night before the wedding that one will seek to transform overnight into that submissive and sacrificial mentality. Whilst it can be an instantaneous shift for some, for others It can take time to acclimatize to the soil of marriage, the lifestyle it demands and the principles that underpin it. This time of acclimatizing is best done before marriage where one undergoes a period of x-raying and uprooting anti-marriage sentiments, behaviours and paradigms.

The period of transitioning from single to spouse is a time in which fundamental questions are to be asked inwardly. These questions can include what key adjustments need to be made, mentally and otherwise, to effect a seamless shift into the imminent new chapter of marriage. The care-free single that does not usually report to anyone, will come to learn that a godly marriage will require a change in this regard.

The single who felt that making herself happy and putting himself first is all that matters, will quickly discover that such mentality cannot produce positive results in marriage and will learn that marriage will require a change in this regard also. If the decisions one made whilst single typically required the approval of friends first, again, marriage will likely require a change in this regard.

So many aspects of marriage will continually be learnt in the course of one's union but there is need to delve into the key aspects of marriage that require a paradigm shift. This shift enables one to mentally and emotionally morph into thinking, behaving and approaching life as a duo as opposed to thinking as one would when it is just one person doing life on their own.

Oftentimes we spend a huge chunk of our adolescent and pre-marital years watching, observing, and assimilating happenings around us which include the relationships around us. We do not form our views on life issues and life relationships one morning. There is a subliminal and subconscious re-wiring and thought processing that happens silently as we see, behold, observe and make conclusions.

In an ideal world all the conclusions and paradigms we develop about marital life will be correct and in accordance with God's blueprint of marriage. However, unfortunately this is not so. The Holy Spirit can help us in so many ways but there are aspects that God expects us to pay attention to, more so than others. The Holy Spirit can point us to aspects of our lives that need adjustment in order for us to excel in the next chapter but the work of self- review, preparation and making necessary changes to enable the single to transition into the spouse will require some effort from us on a human level.

On a practical level, submission involves allowing another to contribute, and in many instances, lead in daily life decisions which one would have otherwise handled alone.[7] It takes one resigning to the fact that complete and absolute control, to a considerable extent, is to be relinquished. This can come as somewhat of a big pill for many young singles to swallow. As a husband, there is so much that comes with being given the mantle of leadership in the home. There are principles to explore, learn, imbibe, and apply to be able to fulfil purpose in the unique office of husbandhood. The command to love one's wife – to the Bible standard set of Christ's love for the Church – requires the place of studying the how behind loving one's wife. It necessitates the study, the digging out, the understanding of what it takes and what it means to love as Christ loves for every single day of one's marriage.

Living as a spouse, particularly as a godly one, involves so many dimensions which can range from the concept of trust, self-esteem, self-worth, general assumptions about men or women, to power and so many other layers. One experience during one's single years is enough to introduce a flawed approach to any of the aforementioned

---

7   7 Ephesians 5:22

areas. For instance, when there is a disposition of not trusting people, or a general sense of suspicion of people which may have arisen from betrayal in the past, this can form toxic cargo to carry out of the junction of singlehood into the lane of marriage.

Whilst purpose tends to first be discovered as one comes of age in one's single years, it is often just the beginning of a lifelong pursuit of purpose. God's timing is so mysterious yet perfect that there are stages in ministry and realisation of destiny that can be reserved for set junctions in your life. One of these set junctions is when you become a spouse. Some divine craftsmanship in you is activated when you are put into a position or environment that activates that divine blueprint coded inside you. Such environment can indeed be marriage. For many the switch from single to spouse will be akin to a switch in the level, reach and dimension of your divine purpose.

A big part of Joseph's purpose found expression when he entered into a partnership with Pharaoh in which he acted as the Pharaoh's eyes, ears and mouth, effectively operating as the land's prime minister. His calling and gifts were manifested maximally and afforded him and the people greater gains when he switched from Joseph the young servant to Joseph Pharaoh's prime minister. In like manner the switch to spousal status can be the part of your story when there is a heightened release and deeper manifestation of the light within such that when it shines, it shines to all whom your new platform will enable you to reach. The Bible talks of this exponential increase in reach when one switches from single to spouse. This indicates that purpose is a continuum that connects each stage in your life and is also designed to have a unique and progressive expression in each stage of one's life.

When the transition out of singlehood is imminent, it is imperative to engage in renewed seeking of God's counsel for the phase that lies ahead. There is an additional need to seek for clarity of the vision that has been allocated to the marriage chapter in your life. This additional need centres on the fact that as part of a married couple there is a fusion of two destinies, two divine purposes joined together. Discovery of what this joint destiny holds is doubly needful. This is because it is imperative for one to engage with and fulfil the underlying plan of God for bringing you out of singlehood and into the marital union you eventually are called into.

Many seem to foster a perception that purpose reaches its conclusion once one nears the twilight of singlehood. It behoves on the young single to discard this assumption and set one's heart unto the fulfilling of one's unique assignment, whilst holding onto the mantle of marriage. It is widely known that the foundation of a house determines how well and stable the house will stand. Glorious furnishings, beautifully decorated walls, expertly designed rooms only make any sense when a house is standing and that with a solid foundation. The single years, the learnings and lessons we gleaned from those years, will oftentimes bear fruit in the spousal years.

Hence why adequate transitioning is needful to enable the house, and all that is within the house, to stand.

Wherever you are in your journey, at whatever point one is at, the pathway of purpose will take one through so many twists and turns. There is so much to unfold that may not have even be revealed to you. Treading the path of God's divine will and plan for your life, adhering to His timing and process is the best insurance policy to ensure that you, whether as a single or a spouse, reach that destination that has been ordained for you from before the world began.

* * *

Questions to Ponder

1. Am I content as a single? Do I sense a call or desire in me to become a spouse in the future?

2. What are my general feelings about becoming a spouse? What perceptions and perspectives do I have about life as a single and life as a spouse?

3. Are there questions I have about pursuing purpose whilst in a partnership as opposed to singlehood?

Scripture Corner

"And beside this, giving all diligence, add to your faith virtue; and to virtue knowledge;"

— 2 Peter 1:5

Declaration: I decide to take on the necessary groundwork required to enable a seamless transition from singlehood into marriage. I choose to not be a last-minute wife or husband who hastily scrambles into marriage with half- baked understanding of what is required. I choose to study the precepts and learn the principles of pursuing purpose as a single and subsequently as a spouse, so that I can carry the purpose-enabling mentality, awareness and understanding that is necessary.

NOTES

-: CHAPTER 12 HIGHLIGHT: -

"Whilst others sought to fit in, blend in and follow the norm, these singles of substance found the courage to do the opposite and strive to be the odd one out."

SECTION 5

THE SOARING SINGLE – CONCLUSION

13

SUMMARY REMARKS

To soar is to ascend. It is to reach beyond, to attain to a greater plane. Wherever you are now in your life, you can rise into a greater you than you knew you could become. You can be that soaring single that epitomises the words of this book. You may not even know why you picked up this book. It could be that you are just barely holding on to the reins of surviving and if you lose your grip you'll fall. It is time for a new dawn. Your new dawn to be specific. A new dawn of shifting from surviving to thriving. From walking to intentional soaring and divine gliding through the plane of purposeful living.

If you are yet to begin a relationship with Jesus Christ. You can today. The Author of your existence is beckoning on you to let Him steer you into the treasures He has embedded in your potential, if only you allow Him to uncover, release and showcase His glory through and upon you. Your purpose is way too precious to toss aside or sacrifice on the altar of indifference or ignorance. Rather, as you open up your heart to Jesus, He comes in and makes life take on a new rhythm of hope, vigour and, of course, purpose.

Perhaps you have taken a hit. You were once making big strides in living intentionally, but a time came when you stumbled. Perhaps you took a wrong turn and you are yet to recover from that. Perhaps you have been busy trying to get through the day to day living that the purpose dimension has taken a back seat. Or you made a terrible mistake and life spiralled out of control and seemingly out of alignment.

You can find your path back to purpose and intentional living one step at a time, one day at a time. It simply starts with a decision. You can decide that you will live a life in which you soar. You can rise into the awareness that you have been placed here on earth deliberately and that you matter to your Maker.

Decide to make the plans, changes and adjustments that are required to reconnect you to the place of commitment to purpose. You can choose today to be more than you were yesterday, to do more today than you did yesterday. With each progressive thought, act, decision and plan you are soaring your way into a truly intentional and purposeful Christian Single.

NOTES

www.ingramcontent.com/pod-product-compliance
Lightning Source LLC
Chambersburg PA
CBHW040241130526
44590CB00049B/4135